Victorian women abroad

Fiona Reynoldson

This book is about British women who travelled abroad for various reasons. Facts about some of these women, taken from letters and diaries, show us about what life was like in Victorian times.

If you are using the book to find out particular facts about Victorian women, you do not have to read it all. Look at the **contents** (below) or the **index** (at the back) to find the best pages to help you. Then just read as much as you need to read.

The basic facts are given in big print, and more detailed information is in smaller print.

Contents

1 Victorian women   2

2 Emigrants   6

3 Explorers   10

4 Governesses   15

5 Missionaries   18

6 Nurses   22

7 Memsahibs   25

8 Summary   29

Glossary   30

Map of the world   31

Further information   31

Index   32

1 Victorian women

Most Victorian women married and had children. Most of them did not have jobs outside the home. They looked after their husbands and children. They also cooked and they cleaned the house.

However, there were some women who wanted to be different. They went abroad to foreign countries to work or to explore.

⬆ Inside a farm labourer's cottage.

In Victorian times, most women married and worked at bringing up children and running a home. If their husbands were rich, married women had servants to do the work, and they spent a great deal of time dressing in fine clothes and visiting friends.

Some poor women worked very long hours as servants in the big houses of rich women. Other poor women earned money by making dresses, selling flowers, working on farms, or working in factories.

Mill-girls at dinner-time.

There were a few women who wanted to be different. They did not want to do what everyone else did, so they decided to go and work or live in foreign countries. Other women went abroad to be with their husbands or to work as missionaries.

3

In Victorian times rich women did not have to work – but they had very little freedom. They spent the day meeting friends and changing their clothes to look smart. Most women had no money apart from whatever their fathers or husbands gave them.

It was very difficult for a woman to get a job, and the jobs women did get were poorly paid. For most women the sensible thing to do was to get married and look after a husband and children. Many marriages and families were very happy, but some women would have liked the chance of having a good job or of travelling.

⬆ A rich family and their servant.

A few women did travel. Some of these women had some money of their own and did not marry. They were explorers or travellers. Other single women went abroad to earn a living. They worked as governesses or nurses. There were also many married women who travelled abroad. They went abroad because of their husbands' work. This work might be farming, or missionary work, or running the British Empire. Often the women joined in with their husbands' work.

▲ A Victorian family.

2 Emigrants

Emigrants are people who go to live in another country. Many women who emigrated wanted better jobs than the ones they could get in Britain. Some of them wanted a new life.

Emigrants travelled to their new countries in ships, and often the journeys took a long time.

On the deck of a ship for emigrants.

Emigrants wanted to make new lives for themselves in a different country. They sailed to countries like Australia, New Zealand, America, and Canada. These were new countries for people from Britain. Some women went to look for work as servants, while others went with their husbands who were looking for work.

Travelling by ship took a long time. It took up to four months to reach Australia. The women and men had very little space on the ship. The richer people had small cabins. The poorer people had no cabins, and they had to live and sleep in the bottom part of the ship.

Two emigrants leaving England. ➡

Fanny Fitzgerald (dates unknown)

Fanny Fitzgerald sailed to New Zealand with her husband in 1850.
They were going to buy a farm.

They were quite rich, so they had a cabin – but it was very small.
It was 3 metres long and 2½ metres wide, and they lived in it for four
months. They took with them all their own furniture, which included
a bed, sofas, chests and folding chairs.

Fanny spent up to 18 hours a day sitting in the cabin reading and sewing.
When the sea was rough, the windows, called lights, were blocked up –
sometimes for days on end. Then the only light in the cabin came from candles.

The cabin in which Fanny travelled to New Zealand.

Fanny ate her meals with her husband at the Captain's table. They ate well,
because all sorts of animals were kept on the ship, so that the meat was fresh.
However, there was no cow on the ship, and the goat died in a storm.
This meant that there was no fresh milk.

The emigrants could not forget that they were on a ship. The noise of the
sea was a constant roar. The wooden planks creaked and groaned as the
ship rolled, and as for the smell – the lavatory buckets and the animals
could be smelt all over the ship.

Annie Gray (?–1871)

Annie was a Scottish servant girl who was looking for a new life. She read an advertisement which told her that she could get a good job as a servant girl in Australia, so she paid £5.00 for a ticket and sailed on a ship called the *David Scott*. Eventually, Annie hoped that she might marry a young farmer in Australia.

How people like Annie Gray travelled to Australia.

The voyage took 3½ months and at first Annie was seasick and miserable. She lay on her bunk and did not eat for some days. Like all the poor people on the ship, she had to take her own food to the galley and cook it on the little stoves there. Most of the time she ate hard biscuits and salt beef.

There was very little water to spare for washing, and soon even the drinking water was stale. There were buckets for lavatories, so the smell was very bad.

When the weather was fine, everyone sat up on deck. Sometimes Annie was frightened of the rough sea, but she was more frightened of her life ahead. There was no turning back, because she could not afford to pay for a ticket to go back to England. She knew that she had to make a new life in Australia.

3 Explorers

Explorers want to find out about new places.
In Victorian times Britain had a large empire.
Some British women and men set out to
explore different parts of the empire
and different parts of the world.

 Explorers would have travelled through wild countryside.

Explorers like adventure, and they love finding out about new places and new things.

Some women explorers wanted to get away from Britain where they were always expected to be ladylike and to do what they were told. In Africa and other places they could wear what they liked and live as they pleased.

Many of the explorers were also interested in finding new plants and animals that had not been seen by Europeans before.

⬆ Explorers would have met the leaders of the local people.

Mary Kingsley (1862–1900)

Mary's father encouraged her to study and to take an interest in his collections of plants and animals from Africa. When he died, Mary had enough money to travel, and off she went to Africa to follow up his interest in the country. She was looking for rare fish and plants for the Natural History Museum in London.

Although Mary liked to explore the rainforests of West Africa, she dressed just like any other Victorian lady. She never adapted her clothes to the climate. She wore a long thick skirt, a neat blouse, and a hat, and she even carried an umbrella! She did not seem to be afraid of anything.

One day Mary was in a boat in a mangrove swamp and a crocodile swam towards her. She picked up a paddle and hit it on the nose. Another time she scared off a leopard which was about to spring at her, by throwing a cooking pot at it. The leopard ran away. She wrote:

> **"I have never hunted a leopard intentionally;
> I am habitually kind to animals,
> and besides I do not think it is ladylike
> to go shooting things with a gun."**

Mary Kingsley.

Margaret Fountaine (1862–1940)

Margaret was the daughter of a vicar, and one of a large family. When she was 28 years old, she fell in love with Septimus Hewson. However, he decided not to marry her, so she ran off to Italy to forget him, and to look for new butterflies for her collection.

Unlike many Victorian women, Margaret had some money of her own. For the next 40 years, she travelled all over the world. She discovered many new sorts of butterflies, and she had many adventures.

When Margaret died, she left 22,000 butterflies to the museum at Norwich. She also left a large black box. The box was padlocked, and there was a note with Margaret's will which said that it must not be unlocked until about 40 years after her death.

When the box was opened, all Margaret's diaries were found. These diaries were made into a book, and that is how we know about her life and travels.

↑ Margaret Fountaine.

Gertrude Bell (1868–1926)

Gertrude was a very wealthy woman. This meant that she was able to travel all over the world. She was very clever, and she learnt to speak many languages.

Gertrude travelled around the world, and between her journeys, she learnt to climb mountains in Switzerland and in America. She was interested in the Middle East, and went back there again and again. She was also keen on archaeology, and enjoyed finding out about old buildings.

Gertrude loved dressing well, and she was always writing home to her stepmother asking for new silk dresses. Even in the deserts of the Middle East, she not only dressed well, but she also lived well.

Deserts can be very hot in the day and very cold at night, so she took plenty of servants with her, and they carried all her china, cutlery, clothes, fur coats, hot-water bottles, and a bath. The bath was made of canvas and could be folded up. Every evening in the desert the servants lit a fire and heated water, so that Gertrude could have a bath.

Gertrude Bell in the Middle East.

4 Governesses

A governess was a woman who taught rich children. She lived with her pupils and taught them in their own homes. Some governesses worked in Britain, and some worked in other countries.

↑ Rich children often had their own governess.

Kings and queens in all parts of the world liked to have English governesses for their children. The governess taught the children English. She also taught them what life in Britain was like.

Sometimes the governess became very fond of her pupils. She joined in the family life, and went to parties or to the theatre with the family.

However, sometimes a governess was not happy. She was a long way from home. Perhaps her pupils were spoilt or bad tempered, or perhaps the family was unkind to her.

The King of Siam wrote to a governess called Anna Leonowens:

"I have sixty-seven children. You shall educate them, and as many of my wives, likewise, as may wish to learn English."

Anna Leonowens.

Anna Leonowens taught the young Prince of Siam.

Emmeline Lott (dates unknown)

Emmeline Lott did not have a happy experience in Egypt. She was there in the 1860s. She went to teach a five-year-old prince, whose title was the Grand Pasha. He was very spoilt. He tore up his food, and flung the bits that he did not want on the floor. Emmeline hated the way that the prince was allowed to do what he liked.

One day Emmeline and the five-year-old prince were walking in the palace gardens. Three gardeners gave the prince some flowers, but he did not like them. He flung the flowers on the ground, and then he ordered his servants to beat the gardeners.

It was not long before Emmeline wanted to go home. She did not feel that she could teach the Grand Pasha to be a good ruler when he grew up. She packed her bags and set sail for England.

Emmeline Lott dressed in Egyptian clothes. ➡➡

17

5 Missionaries

A missionary is a person who goes to teach religion to other people.

Missionaries went all over the world. Several women missionaries taught in Africa.

Mary Moffat, who was a missionary in Africa. ➤➤

Mary Livingstone and Mary Slessor were two Christian missionaries who taught in Africa.

Mary Livingstone had a hard time in Africa. She helped her husband by teaching in schools, and she travelled long distances to teach people about Christianity. She had several children, and she died when she was only 43 years old.

Mary Slessor also wanted to teach about Christianity. She was Scottish, and she went out to work among the people of West Africa, in Calabar.

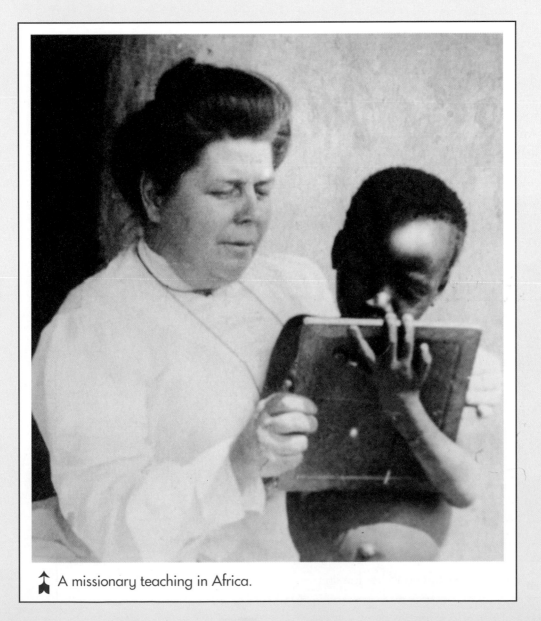

A missionary teaching in Africa.

Mary Livingstone (1820–1863)

Mary was the daughter of two missionaries called Mary and Robert Moffat. They lived in wild countryside in the middle of Africa. When another young missionary called David Livingstone was mauled by a lion, the Moffats brought him to their home. Mary nursed him, and they soon became engaged.

They began married life in a mud-hut in southern Africa, and Mary was soon teaching in a little missionary school. Two years later they moved. They travelled across flooded rivers and through rough country where many groups of people were fighting.

When they reached their new home, they found that there was no food there, and they had to travel 480 kilometres more to the Moffats' home. Mary was so thin that her mother was very worried about her.

Over the next few years Mary was frequently ill. She was often left alone when David travelled and explored. When he first left her, he wrote to her:

"And now my dearest, farewell. Let your affection be towards Him [God] much more than towards me."

Mary Livingstone and her family.

Mary Slessor (? –1915)

Mary Slessor was working in a factory in Scotland when she heard about the missionary work of David Livingstone. She immediately decided to go to Africa. At first she worked in a missionary village, but then she went off to wilder country. Mary did not think badly of the religion of the local people whom she met, but she just thought that Christianity was better.

She won the love of the people in Calabar by nursing them, teaching them, and being a judge when they had arguments. She was called the 'White ma of Calabar'.

Mary liked to live freely. She went barefoot, even though there were many snakes around, and she never wore a hat, though the sun was very hot.

Mary had great faith in God. She once wrote:

"We live from hand to mouth here. We have not more than will be our breakfast today, but I know we shall be fed, for God answers prayer."

Mary Slessor. ➔

6 Nurses

Nurses look after sick people. In early Victorian times, very few women trained as nurses. There were only a few hospitals, and poor people could not afford medicines.

Florence Nightingale was a famous nurse who set up a college to train nurses in Britain.

Florence Nightingale in a British Army hospital.

When Florence Nightingale was young, she became interested in nursing. But nursing was badly organised, and there was no training for nurses. She changed all that.

Some nurses worked in Britain, and some nurses went abroad. Kate Marsden was one of the young women who trained as a nurse. She became known, because she helped people with a nasty disease called 'leprosy'. Nobody would help the people with leprosy, because the disease was catching.

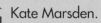

Kate Marsden.

Kate Marsden (1859–1931)

Kate was a trained nurse who went to Siberia to help people called lepers. Lepers are people who have the terrible disease called leprosy.

In the past nobody would help lepers, because the disease was catching. Siberia was a very isolated place, and it took Kate eleven months of travelling by horse and sledge to reach the lepers. She found them living in really awful conditions.

Kate stayed for a few months in Siberia and found out as much as she could about the lepers. When she returned home, she gave talks and raised money to help them. A few years later, a village for lepers was opened in Siberia. It had two hospitals, and a doctor.

Kate wrote:

"Halting at the leper settlement of Hatignach a scene met my eyes too horrible to describe … Twelve men, women and children were huddled together … in two small huts … The stench was dreadful; one man was dying, two men had lost their toes and half of their feet, and they had tied boards from their knees to the ground so that they could drag themselves along."

⬆ Two photographs of Kate Marsden during her travels in Siberia.

7 Memsahibs

A memsahib was a British woman in India. India was then part of the British Empire.

A memsahib had a big house, and she had many servants. Her husband had a good job. He helped to run the British Empire.

Memsahibs having a picnic.

Most British women in India lived very well. They were much richer than most of the Indian people, and they had many servants.

The rich memsahibs had servants to do the cooking and the cleaning. The climate is hot in India, so they often had servants to fan them as well.

Memsahibs' husbands had good jobs. Many of them worked as merchants, soldiers, and tax collectors. They helped to run the British Empire.

In the summer memsahibs and their children sometimes went to a place called Simla. This was in the Himalayan Mountains, where it was much cooler.

 Simla, where memsahibs sometimes went in the summer.

Emily Eden (1797–1869)

Emily Eden went to India with her brother George.

It took nineteen weeks for them to sail to India. They arrived in Calcutta in March 1836. George was the new Governor-General, so they lived in Government House. It was like a palace.

Emily had a busy life. She was in charge of running the large house, and she had to be a good hostess to many guests. She had to invite all the important people in Calcutta to parties or to dinner.

On Tuesdays and Thursdays she was 'at home' – this meant that people could go to visit her. Sometimes as many as 120 people would go to see her on each day. Everybody wanted to be the friend of the Governor-General and his sister.

Emily always wrote to her family back at home in England. Once she had settled in, she described her life as the Governor-General's sister, in a letter:

"I get up at eight, and with the help of three maids, have a bath and dress for breakfast at nine. When I leave my room, I find my two tailors sitting cross-legged in the passage making my dresses, a sweeper with his broom, two servants with fans, and a sentry to make sure no one steals anything. I am followed down the stairs by my head servant and four others and by Chance my spaniel, carried by his own servant. At the bottom of the stairs are two more servants with a sedan chair in case I feel too tired to walk to the immense marble hall where we eat. All my servants are dressed in white with red and gold turbans."

Emily Eden. ➤➤

27

Flora Annie Steel (1847–1929)

Flora married a man in the Indian Civil Service and went to India in 1868. She loved India, and she did not mind the heat. Her first baby died and she was very upset, but she made herself very busy. When her husband was ill, she took over his job, and she did it very well.

She found time to play the harmonium in church, to run the Christmas Eve ball, and to produce a play for the New Year. She learnt the local language, and when her husband was sent to a remote area, she set herself up as a doctor for the Indian people.

She was successful, but she became more interested in teaching. She wanted to help the women of India. She opened a school for girls, and she persuaded the British Government to make her an inspector of schools.

In her spare time she wrote a cookery book for memsahibs. Her husband retired from his job because he was ill, and so they returned to England. Flora missed India, and in 1894 she went back. This time she wrote a novel about India which made her famous. It was called *On the Face of the Waters*.

Flora Annie Steel. ➤➔

8 Summary

Most Victorian women stayed in Britain, but there were quite a number who went abroad. This book has looked at just a few of the women who travelled abroad for different reasons.

Most of the women in this book wrote about their lives in diaries, letters, or books, and that is how we know what they did. There were many other women who went abroad and who also wrote about their adventures.

Annie Gray and Fanny Fitzgerald did not keep diaries, send letters home, or write books about their journeys. We only know about Annie through family stories passed down to her great grandchildren in Australia. We only know about Fanny from the drawings that her husband did of the ship and of the cabin. He also made notes about their journey.

There were hundreds of other women travellers of whom we know nothing at all, because they did not write anything down. They travelled all over the world in their long, Victorian skirts. They travelled in rainforests, up mountains, and across deserts. They travelled because of their jobs, or because of their husbands' jobs. They travelled to explore, to teach about Christianity, or just for fun.

Daisy Bates. She spent many years working with Aborigines in Australia.

29

Glossary

Archaeology Archaeology is the study of what happened in the past. Archaelogists find things out by digging up pottery and other things from the ground.

British Empire The British Empire was all the land in the world ruled by Britain. India, Australia and much of Africa belonged to the British Empire.

Calabar Calabar is an area of land in Africa.

Emigrants Emigrants are people who leave their own country to live in another country.

Explorer An explorer is a person who travels to find out more about the world.

Foreign Foreign means things or people which come from another place.

Governess A governess was a woman teacher who taught children in their own home.

Governor-General The Governor-General was the name given to the Queen or King's chief representatives in parts of the Empire such as India.

Harmonium The harmonium is a musical instrument, similar to the piano.

Indian Civil Service The Indian Civil Service was made up of all the people who ran India for the British.

Leprosy Leprosy is a disease which affects the skin.

Mangrove swamp A mangrove swamp is a muddy, wet area where mangrove trees grow.

Memsahib A memsahib was a British woman. She was called a memsahib when she lived in the parts of the world called the British Empire.

Merchant A merchant is a person who buys and sells all sorts of goods.

Missionaries Missionaries are people who go to foreign countries to teach about religion.

Natural History Museum The Natural History Museum is a museum in London which has collections of animals and plants.

Salt beef Salt beef was meat from cattle that was soaked in salt water to stop it from going bad.

Sedan chair A sedan chair was a chair with poles at the back and front. A person was carried in the chair.

Siberia Siberia is a very cold part of north-east Asia.

Turban A turban was a head covering. It was worn by some Indian people.

Will A will is a piece of writing which describes what will happen to a person's money or possessions after they have died.

Map of the world

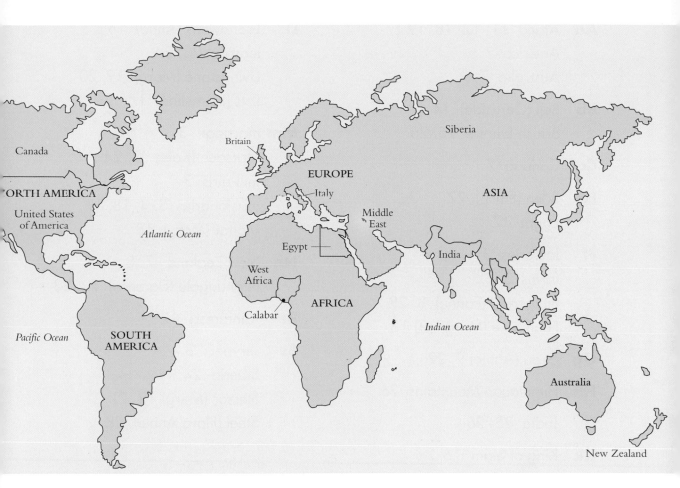

Further information

Places to visit

Castle Museum, Norwich
This museum contains Margaret Fountaine's butterfly collection.

Further reading

Victorian Britain by Jane Shuter and Adam Hook, 1992, Heinemann Educational Books.
How we used to live – Victorians Early and Late by David Evans, 1990,
A and C Black and Yorkshire TV.
Cooks Tours – The story of popular travel by E. Swinglehurst, 1982, Blandford Press.

Films

The King and I, starring Yul Brynner and Deborah Kerr, 1956.
This film is a portrayal of the life of Anna Leonowens.

Index

Aa Africa 11, 12, 18, 19
America 7
Australia 7, 9

Bb Bell (Gertrude) 14
British Empire 25, 26

Cc Canada 7

Ee Eden (Emily) 27
Egypt 17

Ff factories 3
farms 3
Fitzgerald (Fanny) 8, 29
Fountaine (Margaret) 13

Gg Gray (Annie) 9, 29

Hh Himalayan Mountains 26

Ii India 25, 26

Kk King of Siam 16
Kingsley (Mary) 12

Ll Leonowens (Anna) 16
leprosy 23, 24
Livingstone (Mary) 19, 20
Lott (Emmeline) 17

Mm marriage 3
Marsden (Kate) 23, 24
mill-girls 3
missionaries 3, 4, 18, 19
Moffat (Mary) 18

Nn New Zealand 7, 8
Nightingale (Florence) 22, 23

Rr rainforests 12

Ss servants 3
Siberia 24
Slessor (Mary) 19, 21
Steel (Flora Annie) 28

a b c d e f g h i j k l m n o p q r s t u v w x y z
A B C D E F G H I J K L M N O P Q R S T U V W X Y Z